a
Child
is
born

a Child is born

Messages for Advent, Christmas, Epiphany

Edited by John McCollister

Robert J. Marshall
George W. Forell
J. Elmo Agrimson
Morris Wee
Kent S. Knutson
James Kallas
Robert E. Lee
Richard R. Caemmerer
John H. Baumgaertner
Paul L. Maier

AUGSBURG PUBLISHING HOUSE
Minneapolis, Minnesota

A CHILD IS BORN

Manufactured in the United States of America

Contents

6

Preface

A child is born! It happens every day.

A child is born! It never happened before.

One act, so simple, so common, drove a penetrating wedge into all history—separating time while uniting men.

Revolving around this miracle, the church celebrates three seasons—Advent, Christmas, and Epiphany. These three seasons proclaim the birth of Christ to be an act of God, with an announcement of gospel, followed by an anthem of glory.

An Act of God

The main emphasis of Advent is one of preparation. The season calls us to prepare for Christmas by remembering that this entire series of events is an act of God. He is the author; he is the subject.

In his sermon, Robert J. Marshall declares that this message is proclaimed through the good roads of yesterday and today so that all mankind may see the salvation of God.

It is not easy for us to remember always that this was an act of God. Even John the Baptist had questions, and, as George W. Forell mentions, John had to overcome a credibility gap. Yet the true greatness of the forerunner of Christ, says J. Elmo Agrimson, is that he pointed to the One greater than himself.

Therefore, we look no longer "with puzzled eyes", says Morris Wee, but know that this is indeed, an act of God.

An Announcement of Gospel

There was no greater newsflash, no more dramatic headline, than that spoken by the angel on the hill of Bethlehem: "For unto you . . . a Savior is born. . . ." Yet even devout followers of the Christ child may miss the announcement of the good news.

Perhaps the problem is that the birth of a baby encourages sentimentality to such an extent that the immeasurable depth of its message is smothered under the swaddling cloths of the manger. In this spirit Kent S. Knutson writes, "Life is greater than it sometimes seems." Christmas proves it.

The difficulty of removing the external wrappings and the current commercialization of the festival season causes James Kallas to suggest, with tongue in cheek, "Let's abolish Christmas."

For adults, the proper celebration of the Christmas gospel expresses our maturity of faith and freedom as Richard R. Caemmerer reminds us in his message, "In Christ, We Are More than Children."

An Anthem of Glory

The upbeat of Christmas spills over into the weeks that follow with an anthem of glory—a *Gloria in Excelsis* with major chords. The song of the angels still echoes in the sky; the candles still burn. John H. Baumgaertner amplifies this theme by suggesting that the calling of all Christians is to keep aflame the light of the world.

Robert E. Lee throws down the gauntlet by confronting us with Joshua's challenge for the New Year, "Choose this day whom you will serve."

Finally, Epiphany recalls for us the visit of the Magi and their giving of gifts to the Christ child. Paul L. Maier concludes that the greatest response for us can be no less than the giving of ourselves to the new born king.

John C. McCollister

God Wants a
Good Road Too

ROBERT J. MARSHALL

Most of us travel enough to know the difference between a good road and a bad one. But did you realize God wants a good road too? In the book of Isaiah we read, "In the wilderness prepare the way of the Lord, make straight in the desert a highway for our God. Every valley shall be lifted up, and every mountain and hill be made low; the uneven ground shall become level, and the rough places a plain."

For a prophetic utterance some centuries before Christ, the description sounds surprisingly modern. A good road is straight and level, not uneven or rough. God wants such a highway for his trip to humanity; for the prophet continues, "And the glory of the Lord shall be revealed, and all flesh shall see it together, for the mouth of the Lord has spoken."

Building a highway for God must have had special meaning at a time when many believed God had deserted his people. Using a similar reference to glory, the prophet Ezekiel (9:3) indicated that God had left the temple in Jerusalem. Then came the destruction of the city and the temple and the exile of the people. Only after all the suffering did God return to the city (43:2, 4). You and I might have worried more about a good road for ourselves to travel back to the ancestral town. Leave it to the prophets, though, they were concerned about a good road for God!

In our present time, some people have thought God has left his church. Where is the road for his return? Or an individual becomes so depressed or confused, he wonders if God has deserted him. Instead of asking how he can find God, perhaps he should ask what road God will take.

The Good Road Then

In The Gospel according to Luke, we discover John the Baptist quoting from Isaiah the words about God's highway. The story begins with a list of rulers from the end of the second decade of our Christian era. These were the big names of the time, the names of the kinds of people we read about in the newspaper. Though we might prefer to shut out the world when we think of God, the Gospel for the First Sunday in Advent forces us to stand in the middle of current events. Only then does the Second Sunday in Advent take up the theme of heavenly powers. Now we must look to the arena of worldly powers in a text with the most exact date in the gospels.

In John's time, he was not the only one quoting the passage from Isaiah. The Dead Sea Scrolls interpret the verses as a reference to the law in the first five books in the Old Testament. Quite different from John, the citation may still have a close connection. The wealth of history disclosed by the Dead Sea Scrolls is matched by the fresh insights into the New Testament message.

The scrolls were discovered in caves along the cliffs looking over the western shore of the Dead Sea. Nearby on the desert plateau above the cliffs, the ruins of a monastic settlement indicate the place where the scrolls were produced. Besides the quotation from Isaiah, the scrolls contain other parallels to the teaching of the Baptist. Maybe John was reared by the monks. He came to maturity in the wild desert area southeast of Jerusalem where the Qumran monastery was located, even though his parents' home was in the rolling hill country southwest of the city toward the Mediterranean Sea. Perhaps he became an orphan because his parents were elderly at the time of his birth. Records intimate that the monks at Qumran took care of orphans. Life at the monastery was like John's asceticism and placed importance on baptisms or ceremonial purification.

Yet there came a time when John set out on his own. No longer would he be confined to the monastery. He began a religious life that went out into the world. He travelled along the shore of the Dead Sea northward until he reached the Jordan River. Then "he went into all the region about Jordan." He did not wait for people to come to him but went where he was certain to meet the people. John the Baptist lived a life with a destination.

He showed his interest in a destination by the way he quoted from Isaiah. While Matthew and Mark were satisfied to quote only the description of God's highway, Luke includes the goal at the end, "all flesh shall see the salvation of God." The more complete citation agrees with John's vision of his own life. He was to prepare the way for the Messiah. There was a clear distinction between the highway and the destination.

From one point of view, God was coming in a human life, a person so much greater, that John considered himself unworthy to untie his sandals. The Lord Jesus Christ was the way God came to mankind.

In another way, the Messiah was the culmination of God's work, the salvation which all flesh would see. Then Christ is the destination and

John's life was the way God used to reach the messianic age.

There is more. John the Baptist was not alone. All those to whom he preached, whom he baptized, who repented and were forgiven, became the way which was a preparation for the Messiah. People, living people, human lives were the highway for God! That message contrasted sharply with the scrolls at the monastery down along the sea shore. There, the way was the law, the written books that the monks so diligently copied. John certainly considered the scriptures important, but the good road that God wanted was renewed, believing people.

The Gospel according to Luke did not want to record history, merely, but to show the meaning of John the Baptist's ministry for the people in the church at a later time. Historically John had prepared the people of his time for the ministry of Jesus, the Messiah. Later the church continued a ministry like John's. The church—Christian people—showed the way God travelled so all mankind could see the salvation of God in Jesus Christ.

The Good Road Now

It is the same today. God wants you and me to be his good road. When we ask, "How?," the description of John's work provides the answer.

To describe John's ministry, Luke used the word "preach," which in the ancient church referred to reaching non-Christians with the gospel to convert them to faith in Christ, in contrast to teaching those who already believed in order to nurture their Christian life and faith.

Then there was baptism. Historically John's baptism was a purification rite in preparation for the messianic age, whereas Christian baptism meant identification with the resurrected Christ. Yet Luke saw a connection between the two because both involved repentance, or a new beginning.

Although Luke showed great interest in getting history straight, he also emphasized the mission to those who had not been among the faithful. He seemed to say God never converted a person except through another person. John was the road God travelled to prepare other people for the Messiah. The community of believers, the church, was the road for God's journey to all mankind.

Today, in our own land, the church goes about in every possible place, the way John went into all the region about Jordan. There are special ministries to jazz musicians and to neighborhoods where the bars are the chief gathering places. There are chaplains for hospitals and jails, for the armed forces and for conscientious objectors, for recreation areas and apartment house complexes. There are new congregations organized for new housing developments and old congregations assisted in order to reach newcomers in the neighborhood after old faithful members have moved away. There is visitation to new arrivals in the suburbs. There is witness by deeds instead of words only, through residences for the aged and for neglected children, through day care centers for the children of working mothers, through housing projects in wornout sectors of the city. In all of these ways Christian lives become God's way to people.

Overseas the opportunities are even more exciting. In Eastern Africa the church grows so rapidly that some statisticians believe the "Dark Continent" will one day have the greatest number who believe in the "Light of the World." The comparative apathy in the present centers of Christian population could easily lead to opposing conclusions, both equally erroneous. One says overseas service should be discontinued to concentrate on the needs at home. The other says we may as well give up all the new ways at home to help overseas or to comfort those who are satisfied with the old routine in the home church.

We dare not stop in our tracks however. Think what would have happened if John had refused to be God's road. He could have succumbed easily to discouragement. If we peek a little beyond the text, we discover him referring to his generation as a "brood of vipers." Later he was imprisoned. By that time, however, Jesus had begun his ministry. Because John had been a good road, people had begun to see the salvation of God.

There is still a more startling insinuation in Luke's account of John's ministry. The people who heard John belonged for the most part to the chosen people of God. They had reason to think of themselves as faithful people, relatively good as men go in this world. It was just such people who needed the preaching that brought a new beginning. Luke knew that fact as a historian, but he lived at a time when he also knew the need for repentance in the Christian church. The faithful good people were constantly in need of new beginnings.

A preacher today would scarcely have the nerve to call his congregation snakes as John did. The preacher must copy John, however, and remind his congregation not to boast of being the children of faithful ancestors. If we are not faithful, God can create believers out of stones, as John said.

John called for fruits worthy of repentance, for God was ready to chop down the barren tree. When asked what that meant, he explained the man with two coats must find the way to share one with the man who had none. He advised others not to use the advantage they had to benefit themselves. Those who had power were exhorted not to use it to violently deny others their rights. In other words, repentance was not a periodic vacuum cleaner but a way of life by which God moved through changed people into the world of humanity.

God wants a good road. He wants you and the church for his road in order that all mankind shall see the salvation of God. Other people have been God's road by which you have received, without any merit on your part, salvation in Jesus Christ. Now it is your turn to be God's good road.

Overcoming the Credibility Gap

GEORGE W. FORELL

One of the most basic, most shocking, most painful human experiences is the dawn of doubt about somebody to whom we have been completely committed. We have all been through such a crisis. We discovered the father who is not as omnicompetent as we used to think, the mother who is not always reliable, the big brother who is scared, the teacher who does not know the answer.

In his short story "Pigeon Feathers" John Updike describes the shattering experience of a boy of confirmation age, troubled by the reality and pervasiveness of death, who discovers that even his pastor does not really believe in life after death. The process of growing up is the succession of discoveries that our idols have clay feet.

The Gap for John the Baptist

But while this experience is normal for the young, it can also happen much later. In our text we become aware of the doubt of John the Baptist and his disciples concerning Jesus as the expected redeemer. John had apparently hoped that Jesus would free Israel from the oppression and corruption he had observed everywhere. Matthew reports him as saying to the respected Pharisees and Sadducees at an earlier date, before his radical preaching had brought him into conflict with the political establishment of his time: "You brood of vipers! Who warned you to flee from the wrath to come? Bear fruit that befits repentance. And do not presume to say to yourselves 'We have Abraham as our father'; for I tell you, God is able from these stones to raise up children to Abraham. Even now the ax is laid to the root of the trees; every tree therefore that does not bear good fruit is cut down and thrown into the fire." (Matthew 3:7-10)

Now John was in Herod's prison, the Pharisees and Sadducees were doing very well, and if the ax had been laid to the root of the trees it seemed like a very dull ax indeed. So he sent word to his disciples to ask Jesus: "Are you he who is to come, or shall we look for another?"

Again the New Testament shocks us with its honesty. John the Baptist is clearly one of its heroes; he is a "good guy." Jesus says about him a little later, "Among those born of women there has risen no one greater than John the Baptist." This is quite an endorsement. Yet this hero has doubts about Jesus. He is not sure any more.

The Gap for Us

Have you never had any doubts? Especially in our time when we are confronted by so many options, doubting seems unavoidable. But doubts have reached a new depth in our time. In the past in America when the religious discussion ranged from Catholics to Baptists, the authority of Jesus himself was never really in doubt. Men might argue heatedly about denominational differences —but the authority of Christ was not questioned. But things have changed. I spoke to a fine young woman who had been very active in the Christian church, a leader in her congregation, well-educated, who just asked the question of Jesus, "Are you he who is to come, or shall we look for another?" She came to the conclusion that she would look for another, and she claims to have found him in Bahaullah, the prophet of the Bahai religion.

And there are many other options from the esoteric religions of the East to the political religions of the West. Sooner or later all of us are confronted by the question concerning Jesus, "Are you he who is to come, or shall we look for another?"

Thus our text reminds us to be ready for this situation. Doubt is part of life. In the course of the Christian life in our age the question put by John's disciples will arise again and again. We must face it honestly and openly and not push it away in fear or anger.

And this is exactly what we learn from Jesus' response to this question. He does not get angry, he is not insulted by the doubting disciples of John. He accepts the question as natural and normal.

Jesus Is the Bridge Across the Gap

What is even more significant than the question is Jesus' answer. He does not become involved in theological discussion, rather he points to the signs of the kingdom, the kingdom of God. The kingdom of God has dawned because "The blind receive their sight and the lame walk, lepers are cleansed and the deaf hear, and the dead are raised up and the poor have good news preached to them."

To the stern and angry John the Baptist this might seem a fairly pale reply. Not a word about revolution and violence. The Romans were not being overthrown, and the Pharisees and Sadducees retained their respective positions of power. And yet things were changing in a very concrete and specific manner. Jesus listed the incidents that had occurred as a result of his ministry. And they were all incidents that made life better for people, that touched their existence in very visible ways. Last but by no means least, the poor are now included in the proclamation of the gospel.

We live in a time in which churches are split between those who believe in the rhetoric of radical change and those who would retain things as they are. It seems as if Jesus avoids this controversy. He is not interested in rhetoric, neither that of the radicals nor that of the conservatives. He cares about people, the blind, the lame, the lepers, the deaf, the dying, and the poor. The ideologists are always interested in causes: orthodoxy, revolution, progress, the "American Way of Life," youth culture. Jesus cares about people who have specific problems, people who cannot see, people who cannot get around, people who suffer from diseases that make them outcasts among men, people who cannot communicate with their brothers, indeed people who are given up for dead and last but by no means least—the poor.

The signs of the kingdom are that something is happening to all these people. Thus it is the strange message of our gospel that in a world in which we are all constantly plagued by doubt, in an age in which faith has been defined as the constant overcoming of doubt, when doubt has been made the condition of faith, and you can only claim faith if you hold it in the face of doubt, in this world we are given a strange power to demonstrate the truth of the gospel in our time. We can be fellow-workers with Christ, ambassadors of the gospel. God may work through us, "Working together with him, then we entreat you not to accept the grace of God in vain." (2 Cor. 6:1)

We Bridge the Gap

How can we do that? By participating in the signs of the kingdom in doing something about the blind; by concerning ourselves for Christ's sake with those whose eyesight is endangered because they do not have access to adequate medical care; by supporting every effort to save the sight of the old and the young and making the life of the blind livable in our time. And this applies similarly to working for and with the physically handicapped, supporting sheltered workshops, employing those who are disadvantaged because of some physical condition.

We can see to it that those who suffer from Hansen's disease are properly treated and that their illness is understood. We can even make the living dead who are in some of our homes and hospitals the object of our loving care.

Now some of you may ask, "What has all this to do with the gospel? Are you trying to make us into nurses' aides or social workers? In church we want to hear the gospel." I can only answer that when our Lord Jesus Christ was asked to talk about the signs of the kingdom of God, he did not mention earthquakes and hurricanes, the darkening of the sun or the eclipse of the moon. He did not even refer to wars and rumors of war but rather to his simple deeds of love and mercy.

"And the poor have good news preached to them!" What are we doing about that? It is a sign of the kingdom and our responsibility as ambassadors of Christ to see to it that all people hear the good news. In America, at least, the poor are least likely to hear it. There is a high correlation between size of income and access to the Christian proclamation. If we take our text seriously, we shall personally involve ourselves in changing this. For the concern for the poor is a central thrust of the gospel of Christ.

But all this is not a new law which we must obey to be saved. Rather it is the opportunity that we have in enhancing the public credibility of the gospel. I have no doubt that the gospel of Jesus Christ is true. I question, however, that it is credible. But the credibility gap from which the gospel suffers especially in our time is the direct result of the reticence, the stinginess, the sloth, the preoccupation with other things on the part of the ambassadors.

We know how the offensive behavior of Americans abroad can bring discredit to our country and undercut all valid claims of democracy. The phrase the "ugly American" has been used to describe this phenomenon (although in the book by this title the "ugly American" was the one who was faithful to the ideals of his country). People will indeed discredit the validity of the Declaration of Independence and the Constitution because some Americans they have met were overbearing, loudmouthed, materialistic and ignorant!

The message of Jesus Christ has encountered the same problem. We have been the "ugly Christians" who have stood in the way of the light of the gospel. This Advent text tells us to get busy: "Behold, now is the acceptable time; behold, now is the day of salvation." (2 Cor. 6:2)

Why Was He Great?

J. ELMO AGRIMSON

If there is a delay when the telephone operator arranges for a person to person call, she may say, "I am trying to connect you." When the connection has been made the operator fades out to leave the two persons with direct conversation with each other. Not to occupy the center of the stage was the modest habit of John the Baptist. His efforts concentrated on connecting men with someone greater than himself. John the Baptist indeed was a great man!

Great Because He Lived His Message

His personal habits reveal a very simple life. As a Nazirite, a kind of Jewish "hippie," committed to abstinence from strong drink, long hair, simple dress, and the single life, John had devoted much of his time to meditation. His ob-

28

servance of social and religious practice of his community, as well as learning the history of his forefathers made him a well understood speaker. Likely he lived in the rugged part of Palestine. The sabbatical year of Israel came once every seven years. During those months people had a lot of free time, since there was neither sowing nor harvesting of crops. Crowds could easily gather to hear open air speakers like this country preacher. John was about thirty-one years of age when he began addressing himself to religious and social issues of the Jews.

He lived his message because the past traditions received careful evaluation and new focus. His was a bold witness of protest against the emptiness of religious ritual and institutionalism which ignored the commitments to justice, love, awareness towards one's fellow man.

His message presented an appeal to the Jews for commitment to quality of life and not just loyalty to formalities of religion.

Each generation, to find integrity for itself, must ask for the meaning of habits it has inherited. We cannot out of frustration crassly junk them for trial and error methods or life styles. Neither can we blindly cling to the ways our fathers did it. This would make science dead knowledge, politics tyranny, and religion superstition or sentimentality. The dogmas of the past may not be adequate for the lively present.

John asked his hearers to look at Jesus, the Lamb of God. He asked them to look forward with faith in the God of their fathers, revealed in Jesus.

Great Because He Pointed to One Greater

This is the mark of a free man. This was not false humility. This was faith. What does it mean when a young man who could have been very ambitious personally, recognizes greatness? What security and courage made this person! Perhaps this focuses the meaning of Advent: expectation. What meaning has life if there is no hope and no expectation? It means that man is abandoned to his own frustration and despair. Jesus Christ gives man revelation of becoming someone beyond where he is. John in spirit was lifted up by Jesus. John assured his audience that Jesus was a part of the human race. He would lift them out of the predicament of sin and despair. At the same time he was hope because he revealed God from his person. In a person rather than in a ritualistic tradition the hearers in the wilderness congregation were challenged to find God.

Great Because He Knew the Time

One of the woes of our age is that we often wonder what time it is. What kind of world has man made? Will God leave us in this mess? John saw that society is always changing. He saw the failures of the old ways, but he did not despair or give up on the future. He pointed to Jesus Christ as the new age. Jesus said there would be violence, painful adjustment to recognize when new ideas, new challenges, new nations, new life styles, new insights into human experience come. We are more inclined to honor dead heroes (even overlooking their rascally personal record) than to recognize wholesome leaders and prophets in our own time.

Most of the leaders of John's time were backward looking sentimentalists who were better patriots than theologians. Without a change of mind and heart, these men could not accept the preaching of Jesus, who would make every follower more dynamic than even John the Baptist. John represents well the time of Advent because he stands between the old and the new, the old covenant and the new covenant. All of us face the predicament of standing still with our ritual and accomplishments (too often the measure of our failure or success) or looking ahead with expectation because we see Jesus Christ beckoning us to be renewed each day by faith and hope.

Great Because His Message Lifted Men Out of Themselves

Our most miserable days are those when we cannot get outside of ourselves. Anger with ourselves, anger with our neighbor, fear, worry, loneliness, hurts of body and spirit, can destroy us. John the Baptist said, "Look!" He shook the feelings of his hearers. But his judgment did not leave them in despair. As he pointed to Jesus he predicted that he would increase while his own popularity would decrease. Because he had been lifted up by Jesus, John was free. When lifted out of ourselves we find ourselves. Forgiveness from God lifts us from the swamp of past failure and guilt. Love assists us to touch others with kindness. Shared faith in Jesus gives strength to walk further. The message of Jesus' life, death, and resurrection proclaimed today lifts our spirits so that we can increase also as the servants of God.

Not With Puzzled Eyes

MORRIS WEE

Halford Luccock once said that it is an axiom of history that every great figure needs, from time to time, to be rescued from the accumulations which have gathered around him and which obscure his true nature. Take Shakespeare, for example. He is compulsory reading for high school students and therefore often a bore. Then a writer like Ivar Brown comes along and rescues Shakespeare from the classroom and library, restoring him to the stage for which he wrote and acted. Or take George Washington. He is sometimes lost in postage stamps or in the story of the cherry tree. Then Douglas Freeman's book makes him emerge as a man.

Or take Jesus Christ. He was a sweet little Jesus boy in the manger. He was a man to admire, a teacher to respect. He is a problem for scholars. Even a noted columnist, whose writings are greatly admired, helps to blow a smoke screen around Christ by reducing him to "The Man of the Sermon on the Mount." Someone is needed, especially at Christmas, to say that Jesus Christ is not a problem, but the answer, God's answer to men's basic needs. Someone is needed to rescue him from the pageantry, paintings, and poetry and men's fuzzy ideas about him, to get him out of the library and into life. This is what John the Baptist does for us.

Stephen Spender wrote a poem in which he talked about those times when conditions "smother the spirit with noise and fog." What's really important about Christmas is sometimes in danger of being smothered by noise and fog, with sweet sentimentality and pageantry, with party plans and shopping lists, with a soft, pretty story. When this happens, the symbols and trappings and gaiety of Christmas become more important than the message of Christmas, and, in that process, the real Christ is obscured. Because of this danger, the Christian church has historically used the four Sundays before Christmas to help people prepare intelligently for the birthday of the Savior, and has been exceptionally careful to set aside the Fourth Sunday in Advent for the study of the life and example of John the Baptist. No person in Scripture illustrates better than he what is necessary if we are to be able to walk up to Christmas ready to capture its glory and be enriched by its true significance.

We Hear the Promise

John was the first cousin of Jesus of Nazareth and just six months older. He was a strange and colorful person. As a young man, he was set apart by Almighty God for the special task to proclaim a kingdom and the coming of a king. He prepared himself for the task by long years in a desert where under the open sky he could address his soul to God and be stirred by divine impulses that were possible to him in that kind of an atmosphere. The day came when he emerged from the wilderness, preaching and baptizing in the river Jordan. He was the herald of a king. He was the royal announcer of the lord of life and salvation. He was no common preacher. His words reverberated like a clap of thunder. "Repent for the kingdom of heaven is at hand." "Prepare the way of the Lord." "I am the voice of one crying in the wilderness."

It had been a long time since Israel had heard a message like that. John started the biggest revival Jerusalem had seen for generations. People poured out of the cities and villages, down the river Jordan near Jericho and came under the spell of this exciting man. It was not so much his person that drew them, as it was his terrible sincerity and disturbing words. The people were convicted of sin. He made them see their own guilty lives, their need of forgiveness, their need of God. Then one morning he pointed to a young man who was standing in the crowd, "Behold the Lamb of God that takes away the sins of the world," and when the people craned their necks to see this Messiah, it was only a carpenter's son from the village of Nazareth. But John said, "I am not worthy to tie his shoe laces." In that hour John's main task was ended. The king had come. The kingdom was here. The announcer's job was finished! So the crowds that had followed John melted away. He stood and watched them go. His high hour was over. Then, when he spoke, it was to say of Jesus, "He must increase. I must decrease." Just that, but it was magnificent.

We Celebrate the Event

There are several things about John which we may all take with us these Christmas days. If we do, the season will have a new and special value for us. First of all, John knew the facts of his religion. He was religiously informed. He had taken the time to learn the essential facts of his religious faith. No one is going to profit much from Christmas who is not willing to do that. John knew that Jesus, the Lamb of God, came into the world to atone for men's sins: to atone, and in the process to be rejected and crucified.

Christmas is more than just a birthday of the Christ child. It is more than the columnist thinks it to be—the birthday of a good man who taught the Golden Rule. It's more than a writer in a national service club paper says it is—a matter of brotherhood. Christmas is the breaking into human history of God himself in human form, so as to be able to live as a man and die for man. Because of his coming, this earth became, in J. B. Phillips' interesting phrase, "a visited planet," visited by one who came to suffer and die for us. God came as a child, and the baby Jesus grew up to be the world's sternest challenge and man's greatest hope.

The Challenge of the Kingdom

It is easy to be sentimental about Christmas, enthralled by the sweetness of it. Thank God for the overwhelming witchery of it and the mystery of it. But to be uninformed about it, or thoughtless, is to lose the glory of it! The sweet little Jesus boy came to be a king. But his crown was to be a crown of thorns. He came to be the master of men who calls for recruits to his kingdom, and for a full commitment of their lives to his program; who asks men to push open new frontiers for him and asks the valiant ones to be his partners in the task of changing and redeeming the world. He dares men to live on God's terms. Those who accept his challenge and join with him, find that he produces a revolution in their lives, changing their ways of thinking and acting. He makes them bold in the face of life's terrors. Christ brings men into a kingdom, a way of looking at life which makes it possible for them to stand firm no matter what happens to the kingdoms of the world. As one of America's most popular magazines said, "The believing Christian has many misgivings about life but he does not panic or live in desperation because despair is an unforgiveable sin. To yield to it is a denial of Christ's power to save us. The Christian also is persuaded that in Christ God has intervened in the events of human history to make his Son a participant in them and has a personal concern about what happens to the world he has created and continues to sustain. It is his world and God is the God of history." So the Christian stands solid. But, in Christ's kingdom he is guaranteed nothing but danger, nothing but risk and fulfillment. Religion is no longer a cozy, comfortable Sunday morning sort of thing, but an extremely hazardous venture that calls for personal risk every day.

We Live the Faith

It is a way of life, this kingdom, only for those who have courage; only for those who are willing to throw their lives away on a calculated risk. It is not for those who want safety or comfort. It's the kind of thing William James had in mind at

Harvard when he gave his valedictory address. "Be not afraid of life," he said, to the students. "Be not afraid of life. Say to the faint-hearted as Henry IV said to Crillon, 'Go hang yourself. We fought at Arques and you were not there.' " To this kingdom Christ calls us. This is the king that John the Baptist proclaimed. If we know the facts of our religion, as John knew them, we shall be a little in awe of Christmas as we kneel before the majesty of a God who cares enough about people like us to share our griefs, to carry our sins and who dares us to join him in the only kind of living and service that is going to do much good for this world. And if you and I are going to join this venture, or stay in it, there will have to be some honest repentance on the part of most of us because we have not often been ready to risk very much for Christ. We will, I think, be dressing our souls in penitence, as well as awe, as we meet and greet Almighty God at Bethlehem. We will, if we know the facts about the Christian religion.

John was a truly humble man. At one time he was so popular almost anyone could forgive him for a few illusions of grandeur. But John the Baptist had had a personal encounter with the God of history and had no illusions about himself. He knew that life must be used for God's purposes and that he was only God's servant, nothing more. All he really wanted to be was a humble man who listened as God spoke to his soul. So when Jesus came, John was ready to take his proper place. When John was asked, "Who do you think you are?" he could answer, "I am a voice crying in the wilderness." When Christ came, John could say, "I must decrease" and say it with no touch of regret or envy. Now mark this: this man who said, "I must decrease" has his place among the world's immortals. The captains and kings of his day are forgotten, but John remains the man who had it said by the Lord Jesus Christ that among men there is no greater. Think of that! John was truly humble. Pride of heart can keep a man so far from Christ's manger that Christmas is less than nothing to him spiritually, not open sin, not booze, but pride of heart. If Christmas is to be meaningful, a man must be humble.

Two men sit in their home town church on Christmas Eve. They are longtime friends. To one Christ comes in reality, to inspire and reward. To the other Christ does not come. For this one is a proud and arrogant man. He knows about Jesus, this proud one, but only in the curious way of a bystander, and he never quite understands why this is so for him. He is in church, but his pride has locked Christ out of his life. It was no mistake that the angels at Christmas came to the lowly shepherds and not to the kings or priests. In George Bernard Shaw's play, *St. Joan,* Joan hears voices from God. The Dauphin is annoyed.

"O your voices, your voices," he said, "why don't your voices come to me? I am the king, not you." "They do come," said Joan, "but you do not hear them." John the Baptist reminds us that only those who are humble will hear the voices of the angels and be fit to receive Christ at Christmas. Christ can come only to those who know that behind the obvious is the great marvel of the eternal plan of God, only to those whose measure of life is more than themselves.

John was a faithful man. He believed God's revelation concerning Christ and taught it. He acknowledged Jesus Christ as Savior and trusted him. But he also acknowledged the practical aspects of that faith and served Christ till he died. Faithfulness to Jesus Christ is a kind of honesty. It means putting Christ ahead of everything. When the Lord took the crowds away, John did not quit working for him. He kept on until a woman's fury resulted in his imprisonment and death. Even in the darkest hour of his peril, when doubts beat upon him like a storm, John was faithful. He took his doubts to Christ. And so, like all who do that, he was reassured. Like John, we all need the message of faith and faithfulness. We all have trouble with our disappointments and our doubts, but we can trust the Savior with them. In our daily routine, we can serve him with honor. In the kitchen, office, classroom, shop, we can do our appointed tasks honestly and well. In our relationship with others, with our families, our sweet-hearts, our boss, our employers, we can behave as we know the Lord expects us to behave. We can live each day as before God's face, do our best, and leave the rest to him. We can live daily with his guidance and in his strength, willing and anxious to be close to him. We may ask him, as a little girl asked her father when they were walking in dangerous hills, "Daddy, how many flowers may I pick?" and God will answer as that father answered. "Sweetheart, you may pick as many flowers as you can without letting go of my hand." Such faith and faithfulness will make us ready for Christmas.

If we are prepared for the birthday of a king, we shall hear the Christmas bells ring and really see the star shining in the heavens. But better yet when we hear the angel songs which have echoed through centuries since the first Christmas night, we shall not look with puzzled eyes at the miracle of Christmas, but shall see it clearly, with the adoration of those who have found in Christ the Savior the great and ultimate answer to life.

The God Who Comes at Christmas

KENT S. KNUTSON

Everywhere, everywhere, Christmas tonight
Christmas in lands of the fir tree and pine,
Christmas in lands of the palm tree and vine,
Christmas where snow peaks stand solemn and white
Christmas where cornfields lie sunny and bright!

Christmas where children are hopeful and gay,
Christmas where old men are patient and gray,
Christmas where peace, like a dove in his flight,
Broods o'er brave men in the thick of the fight,
Everywhere, everywhere, Christmas tonight.

For the Christ Child who comes is the Master of all.
No palace too great and no cottage too small.

You have come from your homes in the shadows of this night to sing some lovely songs, to pray together, and to prepare yourself for this wondrous night. So men have done for many centuries,

43

in the igloo of the Eskimo and under the palm trees of the tropical isles.

Why have you come? The story is not altogether unique. Babies have been born before and since. Shepherds have been afraid, and wise men constantly travel seeking wisdom. Many still are homeless and children today die young as they did in the slaughter at Jerusalem.

The obvious must never be forgotten, and Christmas is the night of the simple and the profound. We come because we believe that in that midnight hour God was at work and because we might renew our wonder. We speculate about God but we cannot define him. We search for him with our instruments but we have not found him. We argue about him, but the end of the argument is no better than its beginning. But we believe that in the unfolding of this drama he has come to us. We have been grasped by these strange events and we cannot let them go. They belong to life itself. They express life's mystery and they provide the hope for all life's striving.

We can neither discover God nor define him but we can learn of him. What do we learn of the God who comes at Christmas? We learn that God is here. We do not travel beyond the stars or engage in soaring wisdom or turn inward in ecstatic experience to meet God. God does not belong either to the astronauts, to the philosophers, or to LSD. He is in public view in the history of man. He came into our time, into our existence, into the world of sense, of words, of witness, and of interpretation. He came as bone of our bone, flesh of our flesh. He came as our brother.

As little as we understand of what is real and what is illusion, we understand most of all what we are ourselves, and thus he came as one of us. If you would meet God, you must meet him here, in the encounter of one man with another, one man's history with another man's history.

So we call this man Jesus, Immanuel: God with us.

This God who came at Christmas comes in every strand of ordinary life. He slept, suckled, grew, learned, as we all have. He belongs to all of life—the joy, the routine, the work, the disappointment, the wonderment, the crass, the beautiful. Consider all the facets of this story. The working shepherds, the wise philosophers, the royalty, the murderer's knife, the problem of house and home, of travel, of taxes, of marriage, of weary feet, of the beauty of stars, of the feel of straw and the comfort of the breast. God lives in palaces and stables. No area of the human lot escapes him.

Life is more ordinary than it sometimes seems and he knows it all. And so we identify this man Jesus as Immanuel: God with us.

Nor is he excluded from the tragedies of life. Indeed it is precisely in the crises that we prob-

ably know him best. He was born to suffer and
to die. Little children in Jerusalem were mur-
dered for the sake of a king's greed. In another
culture, I am told, children bring dolls to the
Christmas program and when the story of the
slaughter of the children of Jerusalem is read,
they chop off their heads. Bizarre, perhaps, but
truer than the sentimentality which sometimes
surrounds us. Life at Christmas is sentimental
and I love it: the cookies, grandmother's coming,
the colored lights, the fancy ribbons. But Christmas is realism: the power of jealousy, the stealth
of the wicked, the temptation of selfishness, the
pain, the contradictions—all are there. He came
to free us from their ultimate power.

Life is more tragic than it sometimes seems
and he has borne it all.

And so we love this man Jesus and call him
Immanuel—God with us.

But the dimension that rises to the top in this
hour is the God of hope. Life is larger than
routine, than tragedy or even loneliness. This
story is woven through and through with the
note of glory. How does one communicate glory?
What words to use? How better to rise above the
confinements of cause and effect, of space and
time, than to sing of light and angels? Have you
ever seen an angel? Have you ever followed a star?
Have you ever knelt and worshipped that which
is higher and brighter than anything within you?

"We beheld his glory, glory as of the only begotten Son of the Father."

Life is greater than it sometimes seems and he reveals all of it to us.

And so we worship this man Jesus and confess him Immanuel—God with us.

Trust him. He comes to us with an open heart, giving himself, displaying himself, calling you to be what you were created to be, sons of God and men among men. He comes to you there where you are. He will break down the barriers, open the vistas, pull life together. He will show you the mountain tops, the green of the valleys, and grant you a vision. This is what life is for and this is what Christmas brings.

Everywhere, everywhere, Christmas tonight.
For the Christ Child who comes is the Master of all.
No palace too great and no cottage too small.

Let's Abolish Christmas

JAMES KALLAS

You know, of course, with a sermon title like this that I am only half serious. But, let's concentrate on that half which *is* serious. I suggest that there is a sickness in Christmas, a disease which ought to be remedied. There is a profound and disturbing fever throbbing through the holiday which has to be sought out and cured. Unless this is possible, the day should be abandoned and the festival discarded.

Let's Not Abolish the Obvious

Now, I am not talking about the aftermath of Christmas. I am not referring to that psychological depression which hits us all when we sit, a day or two later, surrounded by tissue and tinsel, our budget broken, our bankbook empty, our relatives gone, when we sit alone, blue, almost ready to cry and not sure why. Human psychology is such that the books must be balanced; after a period of exaltation, after we walk on the heights, there is depression, we descend into the valleys. Each year as we get older, this wistful aftermath, this descent into the valley, gets longer and deeper. Dad reflects on himself. His hair is grayer than it was last year. Will he celebrate the birth of Jesus with his family next year, or will he be gone? Christmas, the joy of family reunion, camaraderie, fellowship that we look for all year, comes, and when it goes, there is a silent loneliness. But, this is no reason to abolish Christmas. I would trade as would you, ten years of loneliness to see my father one more time. This is not what I am driving at—the letdown afterward.

When I propose that maybe we ought to do away with this day, I am not objecting to the commercialism of Christmas. A standard routine of every uninspired pastor is to pound the pulpit, and cry out in a quivering voice that we must put Christ back in Christmas because the day has been exploited and poisoned by commercial interests. It is easy to find evidence to back up that charge when you realize that one-fourth of the annual sales of some companies are made between December 1st and December 21st. You can see instantly that you have much rich sermon material here against which you can thunder in righteous indignation.

No, it is not the commercialism of Christmas to which I object. I once resolved never to attack the commercialism of Christmas from the pulpit. I decided that because, in their own perverted way, the activity of the merchant and the twisting lilt of poisoned Christmas carols deformed into advertising jingles actually are forcing a renegade world to pause and to acknowledge the birth of Jesus. The message, at times, may be grotesquely misshapen, amusingly perverted, and yet, one feels that in some way God himself is being served.

In the second chapter of Philippians Paul speaks of that day when every knee shall bow and every tongue confess that Jesus Christ is Lord. Paul is not saying that everyone shall confess the Lordship of Jesus in faith and adoration. He is saying instead that God's power is so great and God's love so rich and overflowing, that the entire population of the world will be forced, even against its will, to pause and bow down and adore the infant Jesus. Despite the frantic haste of modern life, the holiness of God will be forced on men so that even the atheist and agnostic will be obliged to recognize the cradle of Bethlehem. And, in its own perverted way, the commercialism of Christmas does that. Christmas today may, by some, be exploited, deformed, turned into a misshapen caricature, but it is still a recognition that Jesus has come, and a time for rejoicing is in order. The chairman of the board of any corporation certainly cannot ignore the fact of Christmas. It is forced on him. Every knee shall bow, and every tongue confess the birth of Jesus.

On Christmas eve of 1959 our family was in our British Landrover, driving north in French Cameroun, West Africa on our way to the major mission station of our field for the annual Christmas program. As we were driving down off the great Adamoua plateau, descending from those heights, heading into the valley which opened into the flatlands which lead into the Sahara desert further to the north, night was falling. We approached the town of N'Gaoundere—a major African town—where ten thousand people lived. The town was covered with darkness except for the flickering of an occasional campfire. It was like a parable, like a sermon etched out by the fingers of night. My mind raced back to earlier years of my boyhood, my school years, my seminary training. I remembered the Christmases we had spent in Minnesota. I thought of the Nicollet Mall in Minneapolis emblazoned in lights, covered with sparkling Christmas decorations, a whole city bathed in the red and blue and yellow of Christmas, a whole city, despite itself, forced by the power of God to proclaim the birth of Jesus. Commercialism, for its own selfish, self-centered advantages, was forced to write on every wall, "Merry Christmas" while putting the name of Christ in front of every man.

I compared that universal acknowledgement of Jesus to the blackness of the North African village, lying in night, with no light to illuminate it. And, I resolved, never again, to attack the commercialism of Christmas. It may be exploited and abused, but no other day in all of western civilization is so widely acknowledged. The world, the renegade fallen world, despite itself, must pause and sing a Christmas carol, calling that night a holy night, when the hopes and fears of all the years are met in Bethlehem.

Therefore, I have no quarrel with commercialism, for through it, the world is forced to worship the Christ, and every tongue confesses that Jesus is Lord.

Let's Abolish Our Misunderstandings

The reason I suggest that Christmas perhaps ought to be abolished is different. The reason is, instead that the day seems to be misunderstood by us who ought to know better. What I object to is our failure to recognize that Christmas is not an end, but only a beginning. It is not a place to stop, to finish a voyage, to clap hands and shout that peace prevails among men and that brotherhood is achieved. Christmas is not an end, but a beginning. It is the start of a pilgrimage, a lonely wandering that climaxes in a cross.

We would isolate it. We would like to preserve it as an event complete in itself. We would see it not as an outset, but as a goal. We blunder into the mistaken belief that the visitation of God is easily achieved, as if all it took to establish reconciliation is for a few angels to sing at Bethlehem, and suddenly peace bubbles up out of our very pores and all men become brothers! Would that it were so easy, but it is not.

The earliest church seemed to recognize that. It saw with a vision more penetrating than ours, that Christmas, the birth of Jesus, was just that: a birth, a beginning, a start and not an end. It was a time not to settle down and relax, but a time to begin. It was the beginning of the great work of Jesus. The day by itself made no sense and had no value; it was but a start, the commencement of a life which did not achieve meaning and sense until the wooden mallets drove crude metal nails through the hands and the feet of the baby become a man. Christmas apart from the cross is an idle sentimental display of emotion without purpose.

That is why the earliest church, for three hundred years, never bothered to celebrate Christmas. It concentrated instead on Easter, the climax of Jesus' life. Easter became a proclamation of Jesus' victory over sin, death, and the devil. Easter is the beating heart of the Christian message. The apostle Paul thunders out that if there be no resurrection, we of all men are most to be pitied, for if there be no resurrection our faith is in vain and our preaching futile. The end of Jesus' life is the core of our conviction, not the birth. His birth is only a beginning.

It was almost by accident, something arbitrarily thrust on them, that the early church began to celebrate Christmas. On October 28, in the year 312, Constantine was fighting for control of the Roman Empire. The death of an emperor in those days was a signal to begin that convulsive struggle as rivals fought for power, and Constantine and Maximilian met at the battle of Saxa Rubra. Behind Maximilian were the legions of Italy and the East. On the other side of the river behind Constantine were the Roman legions he had brought from England and France. During the night before the battle, Constantine, in a dream, looked up to the heavens, and there saw engraved across the heavens the cross of Jesus Christ towering high above. Directly under the cross he read the words: *In Hoc Signo Vinces*—"In this sign, Conquer." And Constantine did just that, convinced that it was the power of Jesus which had put Roman rule in his hands.

The end result was that Christianity became the official religion of the western world, a role it held for the next thousand years. But, Constantine, in his desire to establish the Christian religion, had to go to battle again. This time his fight was with a rival religion, one even more powerful and attractive to the ordinary man than was Christianity. This other religion was the worship of Mithra, the sun God of Rome. Roman soldiers, especially, worshipped the sun, the symbol of power.

The worshipers of Mithra grew anxious during the autumn when the sun would seem to lose in its struggle with night. The days became shorter, and the hours of illumination fewer and fewer. But, just at the moment when the powers of darkness seem about to win, when there is the turning of the solstice, suddenly and dramatically, the days begin to get longer and longer. The unconquerable sun gains the victory. What a magnificent symbol of victory for an army who worshipped Mithra the sun god. And his special day, the day when the sun began to win and the days got longer was December 25th.

Constantine, then, simply stole away from the Roman soldiers their festival day and called it the birth of Jesus. It was the beginning not of the unconquerable sun, but of the light of the world. It was another example of that axiom which says, "If you can't beat them, join them." Constantine is the one who began Christmas 300 years after Jesus, to turn men's eyes away from Mithra toward the Christ.

Notice, however, that for Constantine and for the early church the celebration of the birth of Jesus was not an end, but a beginning. It was the first dawning of that light which would shine forth in full on Easter.

Christmas was not an isolated event engraved on a Hallmark greeting card where we could condescend to chuck the cute infant under the chin and coo over him and say how darling he looked in his swaddling clothes. There was no effeminate enthusiasm expended over the infant, meek and mild, who had to be cared for in our solicitude. Rather, Christmas was the beginning, the outset, the start of that voyage which pushed back and destroyed the powers of darkness.

The purpose of Christmas was to turn our eyes not to the infant Jesus helpless and weak, but to turn our eyes to the powerful Christ—more powerful than Mithra—whose glory was not his cradle, but his cross. His victory was not that shepherds should bow down with gifts, but that all civilization should be shaped by the glorious news of his victory over death.

He marched to that cross like a king marching to his throne. They beat him, they whipped him, and under that crushing weight of wood and insults, he stumbled and fell. Immediately, the weeping women of Jerusalem reached out to mother him with their tears even as we hover over his cradle. But Jesus rejected their sentimentality and tears. He rose up out of that blood-spattered dust and shouldered his cross. Although physically exhausted, the same conquering personality he had always displayed compelled him to cry out, "Weep not for me, but weep for yourselves, for the day is coming when you will call these very mountains down on your heads, for the light has come into the world, and men have preferred darkness instead." And, he went to his death even as an emperor striding into his glory with strength of such awesome dimensions that even a Roman soldier, the officer standing at the foot of that cross, spoke those words of awe and admiration, "Surely, this was a son of God."

Christmas, then, is not an end but a beginning. It is the start of a lonely pilgrimage which begins in Bethlehem of Judea, and goes on to Golgotha in Jerusalem with the shout of victory on Easter morning. The message which is begun with the singing of angels to shepherds in the fields reaches its full crescendo of power when the risen Lord Jesus Christ cries out to a world living in the blackness of night, "I am the resurrection and the life. He who believes in me, though he die, yet shall he live."

In Christ We Are
More than Children

RICHARD R. CAEMMERER SR.

"Oh come, all ye faithful," we sang on Christmas Eve. A time for children, we all agreed as we recaptured the nostalgia of our own childhood amid the pine and holly. But now fathers mutter, "confirm the feeble knees!" after experiments with new toys on the living-room floor, and mothers wonder who will undeck the halls from their boughs of holly. Let this Sunday be more than a nursing of battered nostalgia. It reminds us that the Christ was meant for something more than turning us back to childhood. For in him we are to be more than children.

In Christ we grow up in the maturity of faith in the Father

Of course, let's not forget so quickly that in the presence of our Heavenly Father it is good to be

58

as children. We are to take his gifts with quick
dependence on his goodness. We are to stir in our
inmost being with joy that we belong to him. We
are to relish the settings of color and music that
underscore the annual celebration of his unspeak-
able gift. We are to be spurred to new obedience
in the family of the children of God.

But being childlike we are not to be childish.
St. Paul uses the illustration of his own experience
as a devotee of the Law of Moses to suggest a
better way. He had regarded himself as a mem-
ber of God's ancient people. He had practiced
keeping the precepts of the Law of Moses pains-
takingly. But somehow Paul found neither help
nor comfort in the Law; rather he lived constantly
in the fear of getting slapped down if he dis-
obeyed. But then St. Paul found Jesus Christ.
Here was God's own Son, whom God put under
the demands of the Law on our behalf. He showed
the way of obedience to God, not just obeying
rules, but reaching out in faith and dependence
on God as Father. It was, St. Paul says, like a
youngster who didn't know what it meant to be
a son, now being matured into the status of a son,
of knowing all the goodness of God and grasping
it by faith.

Is there any parallel in the lives of us who have
not been devotees of the Law? The contrast of the
minor and his status of majority and maturity
evokes a somber recollection. In his last months

in the Nazi death cell Dietrich Bonhoeffer pondered the situation of his countrymen. Without thought they had followed their programs of religious observances. Suddenly they were cut off from those customs and practices. They were like children who had been cut loose from their mothers' apron strings, they were on their own. A poor sort of maturity, of course, that permitted them to condone the evils into which they had fallen. And yet Bonhoeffer could suggest that "religionless" life was more promising than the travesty of childish religion which had played them false.

We watch our youngsters engage in their first religious exultation and we are glad. What is it that causes their childish devotion to cool? The youthful Jesus people are a tribute to the power of the gospel, but a reproach to the churches on which they turn their backs. They seem suddenly to have awakened to a gospel which they had long possessed thoughtlessly; who had allowed them to forget? The church is the company of those who help one another remember what Jesus said and did. As we proclaim and teach our gospel, as we celebrate our sacraments, we sound that remembrance, we bid one another think of Jesus, God's gift of life. So we hope. But where we don't succeed, or where we neglect, we are apt to be breeding slaves to quite barren obedience to forms rather than true children of God nurtured by his own gift of Jesus Christ.

The "comfortable words" of the old Common Service quote John's Gospel: "To as many as believed on his name, to them he gave power to become the sons of God." That is the gift of this Sunday to us, a bonus on top of the gift of the babe in the manger: Don't be just a child, but grow up in faith, be a son of God. Don't be retarded in the parroting of liturgies and Bible phrases, but grow mature in renewed grasp on the very life and meaning of God as your Father. For you can tighten that grasp daily, as God tightens his own on you through Jesus Christ, whom he gave into the world to make you his own.

In Christ we grow up to the maturity of freedom under God

Growing faith is the mark of our maturing into sonship and out of childishness. Faith is that we grasp God with a firm grip. But faith is also that he reaches out to grasp us. The Father gives us his hand to hold, when we grasp it he tightens his hold around our grasping hand. This helping hand of God at work in us, this gifting of a continuous Christmastide, St. Paul talks about in his other observation of the maturing Christian: he practices freedom.

It's interesting to note that for St. Paul the basic fact about our childishness is bondage, slavery. We slog away at obeying God because we are afraid that he will punish us if we don't. We stick to our religious observances in the fear that we shall feel bad if we don't. In it all we aren't noticing that the master whom we are really serving isn't God at all, but our own tender feelings, our own self-approval, the quieting of our own heart. No wonder that we get tired of it all, escape into self-indulgence, spill out into license of the flesh or the outright rebellion of the ex-Christian. What St. Paul calls the flesh, our human appetites uncontrolled by God, finally gain the upper hand, and we simply admit candidly that they were in the saddle the whole time.

Our own land, bedevilled as it is by extremes of poverty and wealth, penury and self-indulgence, selfishness and deprivation, stands on the brink of a massive cry for law and order. We can expect that as people try to feel better they will want to make others feel worse in the name of the common good. We can expect churches and families to return to the slavery of slashing at themselves with prescriptions and penalties.

But we are growing up to be the sons of God! We are growing away from the rule of threat: behave or else! How does it work?

God has already worked it. "God sent his own Son, born of a woman, born under the law, to purchase freedom for the subjects of the law, in order that we might attain the status of sons" (vv. 4.

5, NEB). "Under the law" doesn't mean merely that God asked his Son to keep the Ten Commandments. But it means that he cursed him for our disobedience, he put on him the iniquities of us all, as Isaiah phrased it long before (53:6). God sent him to redeem us, to loosen us from our bonds, whatever they may be—tempers and irresponsibilities and weaknesses, lusts and blasphemies and faithlessness—he sent him to release us from them. The cost was huge. God the Father gave his own dearest and best Son right into our lives to taste them at their worst, to face our sin and shame; and he did it.

How in the world can God's act of making Christ to be a curse for us actually reach us where we are? We worried about this a bit on Christmas Day: what does the birth of Jesus in Bethlehem have to do with us beside evoking some childhood memories? And so now: How does God's giving his Son into death liberate me from *my* selfishness, from *my* fake obedience to form, from the drives of *my* baser self?

St. Paul defines the process: "God has sent the Spirit of his Son into our hearts, crying 'Abba! Father.'" How in the world does that Spirit get into us? The answer is in that same good word that we reviewed a moment ago—remembrance. The Spirit causes us to remember that Jesus came into the world for us, our sin, our need, our joy, our life with God, our maturity. He is the one who holds the good life of Christ before us as lived for us, a pattern and a power. He is the one who through the eucharistic meal helps us to remember the Lord's death till he comes again and to remind one another about it. He is the one who through this action we are going through at this moment of remembering Jesus Christ crucified and risen is renewing his prompting of our inner selves, replacing lust with the joy of service, selfishness with the concern for the brother, apathy toward God with the cry of the son to the Father, "Abba, my Father, you are there, aren't you?" And God says, "Yes, I am here," replacing thoughtlessness and merely irksome worship with the freedom of the sons of God to praise God and love the brother.

Does that make us mature sons, then? Probably not all the way. We live in a maturing rather than a mature life. "It is not to be thought that I have already achieved all this; I have not reached perfection, but I press on toward the goal to win the prize which is God's call to the life above in Christ Jesus" (Phil. 3:12-14 NEB) —so St. Paul described the process to the Philippians.

So, to the people who are maturing as sons of God rather than staying childish, this Sunday after Christmas suggests:

1. Keep on remembering what God has done for us in Jesus Christ, giving him into the world

for us, giving him up for us on the Cross, raising him from the dead.

2. Keep on remembering the work of the Spirit of God in Jesus Christ, as he sets us free day by day, even with many a struggle, from the opposition of the world around us and contrary impulses inside of us.

3. Keep on acting like heirs of God, not just church members or worshipers or Christians in name, but people who have been commissioned by God to be his workmen, coworkers with Christ, learning to give ourselves up in love for one another as Jesus Christ did for us first.

That isn't too hard.

Choose, This Day!

ROBERT E. LEE

Our text this New Year's Day, which is known in the church year as the "Name of Jesus Day," is in the Old Testament Lesson from the Book of Joshua. At first, it may seem a strange choice. What has the Book of Joshua to do with Jesus Christ, after all?

One week ago at Christmas we felt the warm glow of going to the manger in Bethlehem. It would seem that the logical thing to do today would be to reminisce a bit, and try to recapture the wonder and beauty of Christmas; to try to extend it, to get as much mileage out of it as possible, and try to keep that warm, tingly, sentimental feeling of Christmas for just a few days longer.

But it won't work. It never does. By the day after Christmas the tree looked like it had been put together with an egg beater. You have to get up from the manger and go back to your daily duties, and what happens then reveals how sincere and earnest you were when you were at the manger.

So the Old Testament reading for today, from the 24th chapter of Joshua, is exciting and challenging, and completely relevant.

Joshua was the appointed leader after the death of Moses. Moses had led the children of Israel to the very edge of the Promised Land, and standing there on Mt. Nebo overlooking it, Moses had died. To Joshua was given the task of leading the children of Israel into the Promised Land. It sounds simpler than it was, for once they had arrived there, they were beset with problems. First, they had to drive out the people who lived there. Then they had to decide how the land would be divided between the twelve tribes. All the human greed and jealousy within them come to the surface, and it was a frightening time.

In the process they did what they had done across the years: they argued and squabbled. They forgot that the hand of the Lord had led them there. They set up altars to false gods. They criticized each other. They criticized Joshua. They criticized the judges. They turned their backs on their long and noble heritage. And Joshua, an old and stricken man, called them all together and took their leaders, their elders, their judges, their officers, and set them down before the Holy of Holies. Then, feeble and failing as he was, he spoke to the people. He reminded them how God had protected them and brought them through the flood; how he had blessed them through the seed of Abraham and Isaac and Jacob; how he had saved them from famine by sending them to Egypt; how he had delivered them from their bondage in Egypt by sending Moses to lead them; how by the power of the plagues and the Passover, he had delivered them and brought them through the Red Sea and through the wilderness and had driven out their enemies in the Promised Land. And then came these words:

> "I gave you a land on which you had not labored, and cities which you had not built, and you dwell therein; you eat the fruit of vineyards and olive-yards which you did not plant. Now therefore fear the Lord, and serve him in sincerity and in faith-fulness; put away the gods which your fathers served beyond the River, and in Egypt, and serve the Lord. And if you be unwilling to serve the Lord, choose this day whom you will serve."

"Choose this day whom you will serve!"

It's obvious, I am sure, why that text captures our imagination on this New Year's Day. In a sense, that is the problem when you go to the manger. It's also the problem when you stand at the beginning of the New Year. Whom will you serve? Whom do you choose?

At the beginning of a New Year, more than at

any other time of the year, we are conscious of the failures of the past and filled with hope and resolve about the future. That's why we talk about New Year's resolutions. We tell ourselves that now, beginning right now, we are not going to do some of the things we have done in the past, and that we are going to do better and try harder to be the finest persons we can be.

You know the kind of resolutions we make. We are not going to smoke any more, or we are not going to criticize other people, or we are not going to be sullen or disagreeable, or we are not going to worry about unimportant things. Or, on the positive side, we are going to be absolutely faithful in attending church, or we are going to save some money this year, or we are going to use our time and our talents more wisely, or a hundred other things. And you know what usually happens to our fine resolves: they last for a few days or a week, and before we realize it, we are right back in our old ways and we can't quite understand what happened. We really meant to keep those fine resolves. We were sure we could and would; and yet, suddenly, one by one, they've all been abandoned, and we are right back where we were before! That's the way it was with the children of Israel.

Joshua reminded them that day how often they started on the right road, but always there was that turning back, drifting into the old ways, the

old evils, the old failure to trust God! Now, he
says, the die is cast! Now the decisive moment has
come. Now you face the irreversible choice: Love
and trust and serve the Lord, or else turn your
back on him for good, forget him, and do as you
please and take the consequences. "Choose this
day whom you will serve!"

If the issue was clear back there in Joshua's
time, who would argue that it is inescapably clear
on the first day of the New Year? In two areas
of our lives, this is the day and year of decisive
choice! Let's just spread them out for a few min-
utes and look at them as a nation.

The Nation Must Choose

In the first place, as a nation, we must make a
choice. Like the children of Israel at Shechem in
the Promised Land, we have behind us a great
and noble heritage. And yet, time after time,
when we are honest with ourselves, we know that
we have been delivered and spared from national
disaster, not really by our own efforts or because
of our own deserving, but simply because of God's
grace.

When we look at our national character today,
who can argue that we are in a perilous situation?
In our effort to fight poverty and upgrade the
economic standards of things, we are rewarding
and encouraging indolence and idleness! In our
efforts to protect what we call a "free world" we

are not only sacrificing the lives of thousands, but we are winning the resentment and hatred of those whom we have called friends.

In our efforts to protect individual constitutional rights, we may be destroying the foundations of national character on which they were founded. In our desperate grasping, as a nation, for a better standard of living, we are worshiping affluence and leisure, and selling personal morality down the river, and are headed for a debacle such as no people before us have ever known!

We are downgrading honest, hard work. We are downgrading personal integrity. We are downgrading the spiritual strength which brought us to this continent and forged us into a nation. We not only listen to, but seem to exalt, those who belittle and decry the Christian faith! And the question is asked, "How long can we survive unless, at some decisive moment we wake up to what we are doing to ourselves?"

Every great civilization in history has thought itself impregnable. And yet, when you read history, the story is plain: there came for each of them, for Israel, Greece, Rome, the Holy Roman Empire, for all of the others, a moment when the process was irreversible. The choice had been made! Not on a battlefield, not in a legislative body, but in the internal decay that no one would acknowledge.

Our multibillion-dollar trip to the manger is all for naught unless it points us, at the beginning of the new year, to the way of life for which the manger stands! Over our national life, this day, this text belongs: "Choose this day whom you will serve!" God or no god! Righteousness or unrighteousness!

Individuals Must Choose

To that inescapable choice we must add a second: as individuals, we must make a choice! In the final analysis, that's where all choices must be made, in the inner man! Can anyone else make you immoral, if you are committed to morality? Can anyone else make you bitter and hateful and vindictive, if you are committed to kindness and love and goodwill for all men? Can anyone else make you dishonest, if you are committed to integrity? Can anyone else make you slovenly and lazy, if you are committed to the maximum use of your talents? Can anyone else destroy your faith, if you have accepted the gift of faith through the Holy Spirit?

One great soul used to say that this is the "Age of the Great Alibi." For everything we don't want to do, or to be, we have an alibi, a limp excuse, some trumped-up reason. But the real reason why we make the wrong choices, and why we so often fall apart, is that we lack the personal discipline and faith to be what we say we want to be, to even believe that it is possible. The road to recovery for us all lies in the direction of getting down on our knees to ask for God's love and strength to fill our lives, not just now and then, not just at the manger or on New Year's Day, but day after day, and week after week and month after month, until finally the answer comes, and you know that the choice was not superficial, but deep and genuine and unfailing!

The words Joshua spoke to the men and women of his age apply to us, caught as we are in the web of human frailty: "Choose this day whom you will serve!"

Perhaps more clearly on New Year's Day than on any other day of the year we understand that a sermon never has a valid conclusion in the pulpit. The conclusion is always written in the lives of the people who go out to forget it, or who go out to apply it in their daily lives. But some days, more than others, and some sermons, more than others, call for a decision. And that's the way it is today! A man can avoid making up his mind, but he cannot avoid making up his life. There comes a moment when a delayed decision is a decision against God, and against Jesus Christ. That's the dreadful danger we face as a nation and as individuals now, right now!

And the words of Joshua keep echoing: "Choose this day whom you will serve!"

The Lighted Candle — A Golden Prong on Common Wax

JOHN H. BAUMGAERTNER

Our Jewish friends have been keeping Chanukah, the "Feast of Lights." And we stand today between two Christmases, the Christmas of the shepherds and the Christmas of the Magi, the Christmas of the Holy Family and the Christmas of the family of all mankind.

The holidays are bright and happy, bright and happy with lights that are kindled only on days like this.

And so we speak on this second Sunday after Christmas, of stars and candles. These are the symbols of Christmas. It is light that was coming into the world when Jesus was born.

If you want a text for this occasion, let it be this one, in the Gospel according to St. John, the first chapter, verses 6-8, from the New English Bible:

"There appeared a man named John, sent from God; he came as a witness to testify to the light, that all might become believers through him. He was not himself the light; he came to bear witness to the light. The real light which enlightens every man was even then coming into the world."

We Speak of Stars and Candles

It was a star the Wise Men followed, and it brought them to the cradle of a little baby boy, who grew up and became one who said, "I am the light of the world," and turned to the people who followed him and said, "You are the light of the world."

It was like lighting a candle.

In this case it was like lighting a candle from a star, a star fallen from heaven and burning with the light of God among the common, earthly things.

That's the way it was in those days.

Babylon, sensual Babylon, soft and fat on an overabundance of food and drink and lulled to sleep by an overindulgence in the pleasures of the flesh, Babylon was rotting away.

Rome was about to follow, having the time of its life while its armies overseas marched their proud banners before the pop-eyed peasants and presented them with law and order on the sharp edge of a foreign sword. *Senatus Populusque Romanus*—SPQR—the proud symbol was carried and carved into the outposts of empire. *Senatus Populusque Romanus*—the senate and the people of Rome—were having a ball.

Looking for something better than that, a great caravan was making its way over moor and mountain, bringing wise men from Babylon toward Bethlehem, following a strange new star. Their camels loved the soft sands of the desert for which their feet were made and hated the rocky and waterless wastes that drew from them marks of their passing in prints of blood. But there was something that urged them onward when, night after night, they left the shelters to which they had retreated from the blazing heat and began, once more, the hard and tedious journey which, for the masters of the caravan, was the most exciting event of their lives. It mattered very little whether they traveled on slabs of Roman pavement marked by cavalry hoof and chariot wheel or stumbled through rocky passes in shadowed canyons or moonlit mountains. For they had heard and trusted a cherished promise. And they were following a star. It was hope that drew them forward. It was faith that spurred them on.

No wonder that Christmas is a feast of lights and Epiphany celebrates a star. No wonder we've been lighting so many candles. And whether they came from Woolworth's or Marshall Field, they did light up when we put a match to them or held them to a flame already burning. The miracle of ignition took place as the cold candle touched the light that was hot and burning and began to glow with the heat and light of its own little flame. And the table, or the room, became brighter for it. You could see a little better now—the smiling faces of the family, the bright and shining eyes of the little ones—and you could look a little more deeply into the hearts of people with whom, in many wonderful ways, you were very much in love.

Candles are made of very common wax or tallow or any other fatty substance. There is nothing particularly beautiful or lovely here. They don't need to be precious or costly or magnificently carved. Even the heart of a candle is little more than a cheap piece of string. In a dark room *any* unlighted candle is both invisible and worthless—until the miracle takes place and the lighted candle becomes a golden prong on common wax. Now the invisible can be seen, the worthless becomes useful, and the common, even the ugly taper becomes beautiful to behold, glowing with a golden light. Now you're really not looking at the candle itself. You're looking at its gleaming prong, still more on the things on which it sheds its golden glow.

We Speak of a Light

Before a candle can shed any brightness at all, it must be touched by another flame and that other flame must give it light.

One time, in the primordial darkness long ago, it was God himself who said, "Let there be light!" And then things began to be and grow and live, all according to God's purpose and plan, in the light that he had made.

And then there was another time, many ages later, when the world was dark with a darkness of a different kind. And again God said, "Let there be light!" And there was light, the light of which St. John speaks, when, in his own very special way, he tells the story of Christmas. He tells the story of the birth of Jesus as the coming of light.

That's the way the prophet had spoken of it:
"The people who walk in darkness
have seen a great light;
those who dwelt in a land of deep darkness,
on them has light shined."

And this is the way St. John tells it, speaking first of his own namesake, John the Baptizer: "There appeared a man named John, sent from God; he came as a witness to testify to the light, that all might become believers through him. He was not himself the light; he came to bear witness to the light. The real light which enlightens every man was even then coming into the world."

A poetic version of the Christmas story has Mary asking this wondering question of the God who sent the baby she was cradling in her arms:

"What is this flesh I purchased with my pains,
This fallen star my milk sustains . . . ?"

A fallen star he was, fallen at the command of God. Light had entered the world, light enough to enlighten every man. Here was a star to light the twisted cord which is the heart of the common wax in every man and by a miracle of divine ignition bring forth the golden prong.

We Speak of a Spreading Glow

And when this picture rises before me, I am reminded of still another day in the history of the world and the church when waiting disciples of the crucified and risen and reascended Lord received, according to his promise, the gift of the Holy Spirit, and became like living candles, with a bright flame burning above each one's head. The gift of the Spirit had been given to them, the threefold gift of faith and hope and love, and then they, too, common wax that they were, became golden prongs, bright and shining lights to all the world. And so they spent themselves in his service. Like true candles, they burned themselves away, bringing the light that he had given them to all the world, the light of faith and hope and love.

It doesn't happen to everyone. "He was in the world," John sadly records, "but the world, though it owed its being to him, did not recognize him." Not everyone can say, "Mine eyes have seen the glory of the Lord."

We who will soon be keeping Epiphany, the feast of his appearing, we who have celebrated again the splendor of his coming, we who hear him say, "I am the light of the world. You are the light of the world," do *we* hold aloft the golden prong of faith and hope and love on the common wax of our humanity? Does the home, the church, the room, the office, the shop, the sickroom, the classroom, any place at all, become a little bit brighter when we enter it? Or do we bring further darkness into the gathering gloom?

"You are the light of the world," Jesus said. We get that way by sharing the pilgrimage of wise men who followed a star, a star of which we are told that it "went in front of them as they traveled until at last it shone immediately above the place where the little child lay . . . and the sight of the star filled them with indescribable joy." (Matthew 2:9-10 Phillips)

You follow the star, and it isn't always easy. Sometimes it is very hard, but it brings you to the brighter light that shines from the cradle of a little child. God becomes one of us so that we might behold his glory. For St. John is careful to add, "No one has ever seen God; but God's only

Son, he who is nearest to the Father's heart, he has made him known." (John 1:18 NEB)

And once we have known him, once we have received him, there is a warmth and a burning within us and a light that shines from us on others.

It can happen to anyone. It can happen to you and me. It happened at our baptism. It is kindled and rekindled again and again as we touch the light and the brightness of God and of others. It happens when we look for light by searching his Word. It happens at home. It happens in the family, in the congregation, in worship, in dialog and discussion. It happens in prayer. It happens at the table of the Holy Communion. The twisted cord and the common wax of our existence, our being what we are, whatever we are, wherever we are, is crowned with the golden prong of faith and hope and love.

And suddenly all the better things in life, the things that count, the things that help us and help others, become possible for us and for those whose lives we touch with our own, as together we make our way toward the day of perfect and everlasting light.

We spoke today of stars and candles.

These are the symbols of the season.

It was light that came into the world when Jesus was born.

Ever since, this is really all that he asks of us: "Walk as children of light!"

The Kings of Christmas

PAUL L. MAIER

The celebration of Christmas is getting lop-sided in America. The decorations in our streets and stores go up much too soon, even before Thanksgiving, but then they are torn down much too quickly. Just a day or two after Christmas the wreaths and tinsel and lights are snatched away as some kind of embarrassment. Our homes have the decency to wait until New Year's Day, but then the family fells the Christmas tree and looks askance at any neighbors who dare to leave their lights blazing on into the first week of the new year.

It's all a mistake. We shift gears too quickly in our culture, and we ought to let the joys of Christmas linger a little longer. In Europe people have the pleasant custom of celebrating the twelve days *after* Christmas with almost as much verve as the great festival itself, which is what that delightfully silly partridge-in-a-pear-tree song, "The Twelve Days of Christmas," is all about.

Happily, the church year helps defeat this problem by means of Epiphany, the familiar Greek word that means appearance: the revelation of the newborn Christ also to gentiles in the persons of the Magi at Bethlehem. The story of the Wise Men, then, gives us a second chance at Christmas, a reason to continue celebrating, a means of joyfully extending what should be prolonged. But it does far more than that. This story swirls with royalty: the so-called "kings" from the East, King Herod, and a baby king of the Jews. And the interplay of these kings is crucial to the full story of Christmas.

The Mysterious Magi

"We three kings of Orient are . . .", so the familiar carol begins, but already it has made at least two, if not three errors. In the first place, we have no idea how many wise men made the trip to Bethlehem. And they were not really "kings" in our sense of the term. And they did not come from as far away as the orient, that is, the Far East.

But this symbolizes the difficulty in trying to identify the Magi, and some have given up the task as hopeless. In fact, many have dismissed the entire story as a crude attempt to call attention to the importance of the Nativity, a mere literary device mounting a cast of characters too far-fetched for belief. A caravan of eastern sages traipsing across a desert to find a *baby?* Using a *star* to guide them? This would be a nocturnal version of chasing a rainbow for that pot of gold.

A skeptic friend once urged Civil War General Lew Wallace to write a book that would disprove the "fable of Christianity." He even threw out an opening guideline: "Why not begin with those ridiculous figures of the Christmas story, the so-called wise men?" A smile on his face, Wallace took up the challenge, and Act I, Scene I of his book featured the Magi converging on Bethlehem. But then, as he moved deeper into his story, the irreligious Wallace got so involved with his "tale of the Christ" that *Ben-Hur* was the result, and the author himself became a Christian.

Now the point of this little illustration is *not* that the story of the Wise Men is a tool for convincing people of the truth of Christianity. Quite on the contrary: the modern mind trips up on this tale, which may be vivid and dramatic for Sunday school purposes, but tends to stagger an adult's belief.

And yet the historical background of this era tells us that there were indeed magi—wise men, astrologers, priest-sages—in the East at this time, that is, in Mesopotamia and Persia. These scholars, extremely well educated for their day, were specialists in medicine, religion, astronomy, astrology, and divination, and their caste eventually spread across much of the East. As in any other profession, there seem to have been both good and bad magi, depending on whether they did research in the sciences or practiced necromancy and magic. The Magi of Christmas were probably Persians. The term originates among the Medo-Persians, early church traditions give the Wise Men Persian names, and primitive Christian art in the Roman catacombs dresses them in Persian garments.

How many made the trip to Bethlehem is not clear. Tradition, of course, has placed their number at three, probably because of the three gifts of gold, frankincense, and myrrh which they presented to the infant Jesus, the assumption being one gift—one giver. Legend calls them Melchior, Gaspar, and Balthasar, but these names arise first in the sixth century A.D., too late for any authenticity. Other traditions, however, make quite a caravan of their visit, setting their number as high as twelve.

But that a star should have guided them to Bethlehem taxes all belief, so it is claimed. If you set your sights on any bright star or planet in the night sky and tried to follow it, you would be led westward and then northwestward in a great, sweeping arc, but would never be guided to any specific location.

The Magi, however, may have been a bit more sophisticated in their knowledge of the stars, for astronomy had much greater vogue per capita in the ancient world than today. Stars had a profound effect on the daily lives of people in the Near East, who were forever interpreting their future on the basis of what they saw each night in the sky. In that region of clear air, and in that time of poor artificial lighting, the nights were long, and the heavens extraordinarily impressive. It is no accident that the present mania for astrology is traceable historically to exactly this area of the world, and it was the Babylonians who first set up the signs of the zodiac.

In 7 B.C., about two years before the birth of Christ, magi all over the Middle East witnessed something spectacular in the skies—a phenomenon so rare that it happens only once in eight centuries. The planets Jupiter and Saturn came into extraordinary, repeated conjunction in that sign of the zodiac called Pisces, the Fishes. In the astrological lore, which all magi knew, Jupiter was deemed the king's planet, and it symbolized the ruler of the universe, while Saturn was regarded as the shield or defender of Palestine, which was also associated with the constellation of the Fishes. The stars' message, then, was clear: a king or cosmic ruler was about to visit Palestine.

And if the Magi of the Christmas story were also acquainted with Hebrew lore, as many certainly were because of the Jewish colony in Babylon, they would have known that a star was expected to herald the birth of the Messiah (Numbers 24:17). Even Roman authors of the time, like Suetonius, wrote of the grandiose things expected in Palestine: "There had spread all over the East an old, established belief that men coming from Judea were fated to rule the world." *(Vespasianus,* iv). So when the Magi inquired of King Herod, "Where is he who has been born king of the Jews?" their question was not really spoken out of a vacuum, and the story of their visit is not so fanciful after all.

But *why* the mysterious Magi? What purpose do they serve in the Christmas story? A very simple but profound one, for the Wise Men brought more than gifts of gold and incense and perfume: they delivered, at Bethlehem, the charter for the *universality* of your Christian faith. The Magi were pagans, not Hebrews, and the fact that gentile sages performed the same adoration as Jewish shepherds symbolized the universal outreach for future Christianity. "And gentiles shall come to your light," the book of Isaiah had foretold, "and kings to the brightness of your rising." (60:3). And so Epiphany has well been called "The Gentiles' Christmas."

The Royal Monster

The second part of the story focuses on Jerusalem, just after the Magi had made their great trek westward across the desert. It was only natural for them to assume that a newborn king of the Jews would have entered the world in the royal palace at Jerusalem. But for all their wisdom, their famous query to King Herod showed no great tact and even less diplomacy. "Where is he who has been born king of the Jews?" they asked, innocently insulting the current king and implying that he was either a lame-duck or a candidate for swift assassination.

Herod's reaction is chillingly familiar. You all know about his paranoid suspicions at this ingenious query; of his deception in asking his guests for the whereabouts of the baby king "so that he might worship him also," when in fact he planned to kill him instantly; of his rage on learning that he was tricked by the Magi; and of his subsequent order for the massacre of all male babies two years old and under in Bethlehem and vicinity, hoping that the infant "king" must certainly have been among them. To anyone with even the slightest knowledge of the Nativity, Herod emerges quite clearly as "the monster of the Christmas story."

So incredibly brutal was the slaughter of the innocents that some scholars have superimposed a great question mark over this part of the Christmas story, suggesting that nothing of the kind ever happened. But such a crime was very much in character for Herod in his last years, when illness and court intrigue had nearly deranged the man.

It is a matter of record that he eventually killed his wife, her grandfather, his mother-in-law, his brother-in-law, and three of his sons, not to mention numerous subjects. The real villain behind these murders was his sister Salome, who was so jealous of Herod's principal wife that she sowed the seeds of suspicion for years in the Jerusalem palace, concocting monstrous lies about everyone, lies that Herod too easily believed.

The young Herod, on the other hand, had been an exceptionally able ruler, and he changed the face of Palestine during his 33-year reign, erecting palaces, fortresses, temples, aqueducts, cities, and —his crowning achievement—the great new temple in Jerusalem. But now he was old and very ill, with little or no support in his own kingdom. Herod worried, in fact, that no one would ever mourn his death, a justified concern. So he issued orders from his deathbed that leaders from all parts of Judea were to be locked inside the great hippodrome at Jericho. When he died, archers were to massacre these thousands in cold blood, so there would indeed be universal mourning associated with his death.

Would Herod, then, have had any scruples about the lives of a few babies in little Bethlehem? Hardly, especially since he was planning his own tomb atop a fortress near Bethlehem, where, least of all, he could tolerate any seditious plans in behalf of a rival "king of the Jews."

Alas, Herod's final plans—both of them—miscarried. When a loathsome disease finally carried him away in 4 B.C., the Jewish leaders who were jammed inside the hippodrome were not slaughtered but released. And the baby who was supposed to die in the Bethlehem massacre was instead jogging in the arms of his mother on the back of a donkey en route to refuge in Egypt.

It was all a tragic misunderstanding of the infant Jesus as "king of the Jews." Old, suspicious, malicious King Herod was the first but not the last to misconstrue the royal role of Christ. Had he understood it properly and curbed his suspicious personality, he might not have ruined what could have been a great career. Herod's was the tragedy of Othello played out in the ancient world. The twisted monarch should be object lesson enough for us to curb any of the nasty emotions of suspicion, mistrust, jealousy, fear, and misconjecture that can well up in our lives today and make a grotesque caricature of reality whenever we suspect our friends and misunderstand our associates. Burying our delusions is most of the battle toward a healthy personality, and it's no accident that the core message of Christianity is to love—not suspect —one another. Remember the royal monster!

The Baby King

The kings of Christmas come in vastly different guises. There are the Magi in their rich and flowing garments, redolent with exotic eastern spices. Then there is King Herod, rotting inwardly in his royal shell while he waits for word from the Magi, his eyes crinkling with suspicion. And finally there is the one who looks less like a king than any of them: a six-week-old infant, whose mother and foster father had finally secured slightly better accommodations in Bethlehem than the stable where he was born.

The scene of proud and richly costumed Magi worshiping a baby in the humblest of circumstances has etched itself on the world's imagination. And history's most famous Christmas gifts, which they presented, are usually interpreted symbolically: gold signified Jesus' kingship; frankincense denoted his future priesthood; and myrrh, an orange-colored aromatic resin, would be buried with him some 36 years later (John 19:39).

The Magi had finally found their "king of the Jews." Incredibly, this title would accompany Jesus all the way from his infancy in Bethlehem to his death at Calvary, for this was the official basis for Christ's execution that Pilate had nailed onto the cross: "Jesus of Nazareth, the King of the Jews." And yet nearly everyone would misunderstand that title, not just Herod. Many of Jesus' contemporaries tragically confused his role as king. Some of them wanted a political monarch or military ruler who would lead them in a holy war against Rome, and they thought Jesus was their man. Others wanted to crown him a "bread king" who could miraculously provide groceries at the drop of a prayer—like the time he fed the five thousand—an economic reformer who could meet all demand with effortless, ready supply.

But Jesus wasn't a king in any of these senses, a misconception that caused his arrest and dogged him all the way to the cross. *"Are* you a king?" asked Pilate. In his only recorded statement of defense, Jesus agreed, but commented, "My kingship is not of this world. . . ." (John 18:36). His was no political kingdom in the usual sense—Herod's old mistake—but a spiritual regency. Christ was—and is—our king in the realm of the spirit, the one who must assume first place in ruling our minds and lives. For this reason he came into the world. His supreme mission was to announce the "Kingdom of God"—God's rule among people—so that we also might take up heavenly citizenship through the naturalization papers of faith. So that we could pray in that most famous prayer, "Your kingdom come"—may your rule as king be established *in us*.

The Kings of Christmas, then, is an open-ended story, for something began with the visit of the Wise Men that has never stopped. True, after their adoration in Bethlehem, the Magi remounted their ungainly camels and disappeared from history, leaving a multitude of questions in their wake. But they did achieve their purpose in the total story of Christmas, which was to expand it. Up to now, the Nativity had been highly local in nature: only a few people of the lower classes of just one nationality had been involved—those famous men on the night shift, the shepherds. But the visit of the eastern "kings" burst all that, as rich gentiles joined poor Jews, as King Herod and the priestly establishment at Jerusalem became concerned, and even the stars looked in.

And the whole world has been looking in ever since. It has not always understood the baby correctly. There would be many Herods after Herod. But at the close of these "twelve days of Christmas," let's rather take our cue from the eastern sages as we approach the infant monarch of Epiphany. Before entering the humble house, let's first deposit outside all the burdens that accompanied us on the long trek to Bethlehem—the whole dusty sin complex, heavy with all its shabby complications—and then drop to our knees in gratitude before the newborn Christ. Let's each offer up a gift of appreciation for the forgiveness pledged in his mission for us: ourselves. For this is the way we renew our pledge of allegiance to the baby king.

Additional Resources

from Augsburg

THE FOURTH CANDLE

Messages for Advent, Christmas and Epiphany
by Per Lønning
trans. by O. G. Malmin

Eleven fresh and stimulating sermons for the Advent-Christmas season applying the festival messages to the present day and bringing biblical truths into meaningful experiences for modern man. 112 pages. Paper.
Code 10-2360

LET US ADORE HIM

Dramas and Meditations for Advent, Christmas, Epiphany
by W. A. Poovey

Thousands have enjoyed Poovey's plays on Lenten themes and on parables. Now he turns his attention to the messages of Advent, Christmas, and Epiphany and creatively interprets the expectation, the joy, and the fulfillment presented by this portion of the church year. 128 pages. Paper.
Code 10-3820

MUSTARD SEEDS AND WINESKINS

Dramas and Meditations on Seven Parables
by W. A. Poovey

The dynamic encounter between contemporary drama and the biblical message of the parables is presented on these pages. The Jesus who told these parables to people in the first century encounters listeners today through this fresh and stimulating interpretation. 128 pages. Paper.
Code 10-4565

THE WONDER OF BEING LOVED

Messages for Lent and Every Season

by Alvin N. Rogness

In this book Rogness expresses his own wonder at being loved. He explores the mystery that God continues to be gracious despite man's failure and rebellion. He sees possibilities for bridging the gap between man and God through forgiveness, hope for the future in the love of God, and a wonderful new life style characterized by love, joy, peace, and faith. 72 pages. Paper.
Code 10-7265

GOD'S DRAMA IN SEVEN ACTS

Meditations on the Words of Christ from the Cross

by Kent S. Knutson

This Lenten devotional book brings Christ's words from the cross into everyday living by interpreting them in the light of his life. A meaningful personal devotional as well as a source of sermon ideas. 48 pages. Paper.
Code 10-2660

FRIENDS IN THE UNDERGROUND CHURCH

Sermons for Lent and Easter

by John H. Baumgaertner

These nine Lenten sermons bring to life the "friends" Paul mentions in the closing chapter of his letter to the Romans. We feel a kinship with them and discover that now, as then, the church is people—all kinds of people—united by faith and love. 128 pages. Paper.
Code 10-2390

THE GARDEN AND THE GRAVEYARD

Sermons on Genesis for Lent and Easter

by George M. Bass

These nine sermons present a refreshing view of Lent. They deal with the predicaments man has created—population crisis, pollution, war and murder—but always in light of the redemptive and saving action of God. The Garden, not the Graveyard is the basis for these Lenten sermons. 96 pages. Paper.
Code 10-2530

Date

Code 4386-04, CLS-4, Broadman Supplies, Nashville, Tenn.,
Printed in U.S.A.